The Decluttering Game

Downsize Your Home

While Upsizing Your Fun.

Ready, Set, Go!

Sejal Parekh and Paula Keane

ISBN-13: 978-1-64184-336-2 (hardback)

ISBN-13: 978-1-64184-337-9 (ebook)

Table of Contents

Introduction

Hello! Are you looking for a fun family activity that will also help put your house in order? If so, you are in the right place!

I'm Sejal Parekh, a home stager, interior designer, and decluttering enthusiast. I have written this book along with my good friend Paula Keane who was a Professional Organizer for thirty years. We love helping people get their clutter out the door and donating it to worthy causes!

I discovered the magic of decluttering as I went from a certified pack rat to creating a clutter-free life. It started by giving a few things away. I loved the feeling it gave me and over time, I strengthened my decluttering muscle. Paula started decluttering to help overwhelmed people let go of their clutter while providing them moral support.

You can read more about each of our stories and some of the great benefits of decluttering at www.thedeclutteringgame.com.

To make things fun, we are going to turn decluttering into a game! There are five "rounds" and each "round" has a timed challenge. You will have anywhere from 40 to 60 minutes for each challenge.

You can do these challenges all in one day, over a weekend, or do one challenge per day over a week. You can focus on specific rooms and then do the rounds again with different rooms in mind. Or you can tackle your entire home in each round. Feel free to play these rounds multiple times and watch as everyone finds more things they are ready to let go of!

What You'll Need to Play

OK, let's get things started! Your first job is to gather as a group and decide on a day and time that everyone is free to play. This game can also be played solo. To make it more fun, call a friend or relative and play against them, competing virtually and share results via text or phone. Be sure to wear comfortable clothes on game day so you can easily search high and low to find your clutter.

Here are the items you will need to play:

- This book
- A piece of paper and pen or smartphone
- A timer (or you can use your smartphone)
- 6 large boxes or 6 large Hefty-sized garbage bags (or paper grocery bags)
- A sheet or blanket
- Sticky notes
- Marker
- Upbeat music

- A tray full of snacks (cookies, chips, veggies and dip, etc.)

- Some refreshing drinks (tea, coffee, lemonade, juice, etc.)

- Family members ready to play!

The Decluttering Game

Instructions

Step 1

Gather all of the players in a central room of your home – I would recommend either the living room or dining room. Select a scorekeeper. On a piece of paper or on a smartphone, have the scorekeeper write down each person's name in alphabetical order. For each item that is brought back at the end of the round, the player earns a point. You will be tallying the number of **"Decluttering Points"** each person earns after each round. *The person with the most points at the end of the five rounds wins!* As a group, pick a fun prize for the person who wins the game!

Step 2

Place the large boxes or large garbage bags in a row in an open area of the room. This area is considered **Home Base** and it is where each person will bring their collected items. Label the boxes or bags with the following categories: **Donation, Returns, Borrowed Items, Shredding, Trash,** and **Possible Donation.** If you don't have boxes or bags or prefer to lay everything out on the ground, lay down a sheet or blanket to mark the area where your decluttered items will be placed. Write the six labels on sticky notes and spread them out on the sheet or blanket.

Step 3

Come up with a 30-second group happy dance! This is going to be your celebration dance after you finish each round (and believe me, you will want to celebrate!). It can be a dance everyone does to a favorite song or freestyle dance moves for 30 seconds. Be creative and get your juices flowing!

Step 4

Create a fun snack tray with your choice of favorite snacks and drinks. Place it somewhere near **Home Base** or in the kitchen. Pull together some fun foods like cookies, cheese and crackers, fruits, chocolate, or chips and salsa as well as juice, iced tea, coffee, or smoothies. These refreshments will give you an energy boost as you get ready to play the next round!

Step 5

Select a DJ and create a playlist of everyone's favorite songs. One of the magic ingredients of decluttering is raising your energy level and the perfect way to do that is with upbeat and happy music. The DJ will start the music at the beginning of each round.

Step 6

Give each player a paper grocery bag (or two) or other container such as a box, laundry basket, garbage bag, etc. to collect their items.

Let's Start: Team Huddle!

Pick someone in the group to read the following out loud:

Welcome everyone. I hope you are ready to declutter! Before we start, let's take a second to think through what exactly is clutter?

Clutter is a drawer full of mismatched socks, clothes and shoes you no longer wear, or knick-knacks spread throughout your home. Clutter can be piles of paper, craft supplies, unread books, or boxes in the garage with things you haven't looked at in years. Clutter is anything you have too much of, don't use, don't want, or don't need. It takes up space and can weigh you down. As you get ready to play this game, *give yourself permission to let this stuff go!* It will free you in the most incredible way.

There are five rounds in this game. Each round has a **Challenge** and an explanation of **Why**. As you listen to the **Why** being read aloud, imagine what things you will declutter. Once the challenge is read, start the timer, start the music, and head toward your room or any space in the home to collect clutter!

When the timer goes off, the round is done. Gather all the items you have collected and bring them back to **Home Base**. Have the scorekeeper tally each person's items and record the total next to each player's name. Put the items in the appropriate **Home Base** boxes or bags.

When all the points have been added up for that round, take a look at the items you have decluttered! Do your happy dance and celebrate with a 10-minute snack break. Select a new person to read the next round's challenge, start the music, set the timer, and **go, go, go!**

ROUND 1

Pick a player to read the following instructions out loud including Why:

Challenge: Gather any duplicate items that you no longer need.

Time limit: 40 minutes

Why? One big source of clutter is holding on to multiples of things you don't need or use. Think about what items you may have that are repeats. The problem with keeping all of these extra items is that they take up physical and mental space. Gather these (and only these!) items in this round and bring them back to **Home Base**.

Start the music, set the timer, and GO!

End of Round 1: Take a look at the items each person brought back and add them to the appropriate boxes or bags. The scorekeeper will record everyone's scores. How did you do?

Do your Happy Dance and take a snack break.

Pat yourselves on the back for a fabulous job! You are now ready for Round 2.

ROUND 2

Pick a player to read the following instructions out loud including Why:

Challenge: Gather anything you've been collecting that no longer brings you happiness.

Time limit: 45 minutes

Why? Collections! You may be collecting a certain item knowingly or unknowingly. People collect all sorts of things from knick knacks and baseball cards to vintage dishes and designer sneakers. We get excited about creating a collection and before you know it, the collection ends up taking up valuable space and having a life of its own. Go through any items you are collecting and keep only the ones that truly bring you happiness. Bring the rest back to Home Base.

Start the music, set the timer, and GO!

End of Round 2: Gather back at **Home Base** and enter your latest scores. Move all the collected items to the appropriate boxes or bags.

Do your Happy Dance and enjoy a ten minute snack break.

Way to go! Get ready for Round 3.

ROUND 3

Pick a player to read the following instructions out loud including Why:

Challenge: Gather any gifts you don't use and are keeping because of sentiment or guilt.

Time limit: 45 minutes

Why? We often become paralyzed when it comes to letting go of gifts. It is fun to receive gifts but we often have a hard time giving ourselves permission to let them go at some point. Out of guilt, we may feel like we have to keep them forever. You don't! Gifts come into our homes every year. You may not realize it but over time, they accumulate and lead to clutter. To maintain a balance, be liberal about letting go of gifts when they are no longer useful, and you will magically create some open space!

Go through your home and find any gifts you are ready to part with. Think of the person who gave you that gift and know that they will be ok if you let it go. If you want to remember it, take a picture of it on your phone as a memory. Bring the gifts you've collected back to **Home Base**.

Start the music, set the timer, and GO!

End of Round 3: Gather back at **Home Base** and enter your latest scores. Add the gifts each person has collected to the appropriate boxes or bags.

You know what to do - do your Happy Dance and take ten for snack time!

You are on fire! Now it's time for Round 4.

ROUND 4

Pick a player to read the following instructions out loud including Why:

Challenge: Gather or tag anything you are ready to sell.

Time limit: 60 minutes

Why? When we are thinking about selling or donating something, what often stops us is the thought that we may need it one day. One great way to get over this fear is to be able to earn some money for those items and sell them to someone who can use them. There are numerous websites and apps that help make this easy.

In this round, give each person some post-its and a marker or pen. Walk through your home and put a post-it on any large item you would like to sell and for how much. This can include things such as a desk, bookshelf, stationary bike, etc. For any small or medium-sized items that you would like to sell, find an open area in your home and gather them there.

Start the music, set the timer, and GO!

End of Round 4: Gather back at **Home Base** and enter your latest scores for large, medium, and small items each person has designated to sell. Now take 20 minutes to photograph each item and post on Facebook Marketplace, NextDoor.com, or any online selling app you prefer to use.

Once you post the first item and receive a response, you will feel the excitement and momentum to post more.

Word of caution: when using any selling apps or websites, be cautious with your personal information and address and only plan to meet buyers during daylight hours somewhere safe such as a police station or public space.

Way to go! It's time to do your Happy Dance and enjoy a well-deserved snack break.

Now you're burning! Proceed to Round 5.

ROUND 5

Pick a player to read the following instructions out loud including Why:

Challenge: Pick one of these categories to tackle for the final round: papers, clothes, or books.

Time limit: 60 minutes

This round is your final round! You have strengthened your decluttering muscles in the previous four rounds and now you are ready to put all of your skills into action. Read below for the instructions in each category.

Papers: For papers, gather all loose papers and unprocessed mail. Quickly sort into: papers to keep and file, papers to shred, papers to recycle, and papers that need to be addressed. Bring the shredding and recycling papers back to Home Base. Find a small basket or tray to collect important mail and papers that need further action.

Clothes: Use this allotment of time to go through your clothes. Remove all the clothes from your closet and lay them on your bed. Sort this pile into clothes that do not fit, clothes you no longer wear, and clothes you need to return to the store. In addition, do the

16

same sorting with your shoes, socks, scarves, and accessories. If there are any clothes you want to try on, set them aside in a container of your choice (a shopping bag, basket, etc.) and try them on when you have the time.

Books: Go to where you store your books whether they are in your bedroom, an office, or maybe on bookshelves. Sort all of your books into the following categories: books you no longer want to read, books you may not reference again, and books you are ready to give away. Focus on keeping only the books you are excited to read or those that you frequently reference. Bring the remaining books back to **Home Base**.

Start the music, set the timer, and GO!

End of Round 5: Gather back at **Home Base** and enter your latest scores. Fill the appropriate boxes or bags with all of the items you have gathered.

You did it! Each of you completed the 5 rounds of The Decluttering Game. Take a look at all of the items you have gathered. Applaud yourselves for becoming Clutter Warriors. Take a photo, post on social media with #thedeclutteringgame" and tag us so we can see your incredible work!

Add up everyone's scores and determine the winner. Give the winner a round of applause! Do your Happy Dance and take a well-deserved snack break. If the weather is nice, open up your windows and let the fresh air and sunshine pour in and rejuvenate your home.

You can always play this game again to keep the decluttering momentum going!

Some Fun Decluttering Tips

Now that you have completed The Decluttering Game, here are a few more decluttering tips to try!

Tip 1: Have a easy-to-find donation box in your home. Place a donation box in a closet or in a corner of your garage. This will make it fun and easy for family members to drop in their donation items. When the box is full, make a trip to drop off the items at your favorite charity.

Tip 2: Surprise a friend or relative. For unused or very lightly used items that you don't see yourself using such as books, jewelry, gardening tools, craft supplies, toys, etc, one fun and unexpected thing you can do is grab a few of these items, pack them in a bag, and surprise a friend or family member who might enjoy them (maybe an avid reader, gardener, or crafter). You just might make their day!

Tip 3: Share your decluttering philosophy. When you give your friends and family a gift, let them know it's ok to give it away. You can say, "feel free to pass this along if it's not the right thing for you." It makes for a laugh and is a light-hearted way to tell them you don't expect them to keep it forever! You can say it verbally or include a note or funny poem with your gift.

Tip 4: Host a clutter exchange party. Invite friends and family and have them bring their extra unneeded items (e.g. kids clothing, toys, gifts, and sports equipment). Think of it as creating a vintage thrift boutique. Provide snacks and drinks and enjoy socializing while everyone shops. Don't forget to take pictures! Whatever remains at the end of the event, you can donate.

Decluttering Inspiration
A Few Great
Blogs and Books

For a little more inspiration, here are some of my favorite decluttering blogs and books.

- Becoming Minimalist – Joshua Becker
  www.becomingminimalist.com

- Be More with Less – Courtney Carver
  www.bemorewithless.com

- Zen Habits – Leo Babauta
  www.zenhabits.net

- Apartment Therapy
  www.apartmenttherapy.com

- Book: *The Life Changing Art of Tidying Up* by
  Marie Kondo

- Book: *Let It Go* by Peter Walsh (or any other book by Peter Walsh)

- Book: *The Power of Less* by Leo Babauta

Where to Donate Your Items

Here are a few ideas for where to donate your items: non-profit organization, homeless shelter (for various household items), animal shelter/veterinarian's office (for extra linens and towels), library (for books), and food bank (for unexpired dry foods and canned goods). Check with friends and family to see if they know of any groups needing donations. Be resourceful and creative while helping your community!

For heavy items that need to be hauled away, look up your local trash or junk hauling company. If you have a lot of paper to be shred, look up local shredding companies where you can drop it off. Items such as old paint can often be taken to paint supply stores for disposal.

Share Your Success

We'd love for you to share your decluttering tips, a-ha moments, and photos dropping off your donation items. You never know who it might inspire.

If you found this book fun and helpful, share it on social media and tell your friends about it. Use the hashtag #thedeclutteringgame. And we'd love to connect with you on the social platforms below.

Here's wishing you incredible success as you simplify your life. Remember, decluttering is the name of the game!

Ready, Set, Go!

Sejal and Paula

@sejal_parekh

www.facebook.com/innovaedesigns

www.innovaedesigns.com
www.thedeclutteringgame.com

Acknowledgments

I am deeply grateful to the following people who have helped make this book possible! Thank you Paula for our friendship, hours of decluttering and laughs while doing so, and for your help and insight with this book. What a treat to work on this together.

Thank you to Chris O'Byrne, Debbie O'Byrne, and the team at JETLAUNCH.net for your excellent work and for helping bring this idea to life. More importantly, thank you for being so enjoyable to work with!

Thank you to my sister, Neetal Parekh, for your enthusiasm, ideas, and unwavering support of projects big and small.

Thank you to my friends, family, and colleagues- Alice, Amita, Beth, BJ, Cindy, Eri, Gulalai, Gus, Jackie, James, Javier, Karen, Lena, Linda, Margie, Miyuki, Nancy, Nashua, Nina, Sandy, Stephanie, Suzanne, Terri, Tracey, and Virginia. I am truly grateful for your friendship, support, and editing when needed!

Thank you to my family - Dad, Neetal, Sunil, Bhupinder, Sukhman, Jodhveer, Nani, and extended family for your love and support. To my mom, we've turned your love of an organized home into a game!

Thank you to the incredible real estate agents, brokers, clients, and partner vendors we work side by side with.

To the readers of this book, thank you for taking a chance and playing this game. I hope in some small way, it changes your life.

www.ingramcontent.com/pod-product-compliance
Lightning Source LLC
Chambersburg PA
CBHW070757050426
42452CB00010B/1871